The Best of
Singaporean Cooking

THE BEST OF SINGAPOREAN COOKING

Published in the United Kingdom by
CENTURION BOOKS LIMITED
52 George Street London W1H 5RF

British Library Cataloguing in Publication Data

Mitchell, John
  Best of Singaporean cooking
  I.Title
  641.595955
  ISBN 0948500069 *Paperback*

Photo credits:
Michael Freeman: Cover, Pages 25 ,38, 43, 50, 56, 61, 69 and 72
Benno Gross: Pages 8, 12, 13, 20, 21, 26, 30, 31, 32, 37, 49, 54, 55,
    64, 70, 71, 77 and 80
David Cornwell: Pages 16 and 36
Harold Teo: Page 44
Photos on pages 1, 4, 6 and 7 are courtesy of the
    Singapore Tourist Promotion Board.

Design and Artwork supplied by Centurion Design Forum Ltd.
Printed in China by Twin Age Limited

The Best of Singaporean Cooking

John Mitchell

A selection of Singapore's favourite recipes

CENTURION

Contents

Introduction

The first person to describe Singapore as "The Crossroads of Asia", no doubt had in mind its geographical location situated, as it is, practically on the equator at the very heart of South East Asia, with easy accessibility to China and Japan to the north and the Indian sub-continent to the west. Yet how aptly this same phrase can be taken to introduce the culinary delights of this colourful and compact Island State where the visitor is greeted with an amazing variety of tangy aromas and spicy flavours which so accurately reflect the varied racial origins of today's Singaporeans.

In the kitchens of Singapore the many styles of Chinese cooking compete with the richly-spiced foods of the Malays and Indians. Here, a multitude of cooks manage not only to successfully reproduce the traditional fare of their ancestors but also to create new and exciting recipes by 'blending cuisines' like others elsewhere blend spices.

Since people of Chinese origin predominate so does their food. From the highly-esteemed flavours of the south to the fiery tastes of Szechuan and from the classical cooking of Imperial Peking to the simple food of the wandering Hakkas, dishes from all the regions of China are prepared and enjoyed in homes and restaurants throughout Singapore. And then there are all the marvellous curries; the coconut-flavoured curries of neighbouring Malaysia, the biting curries of southern India, the more subtle tastes from the north and even the milder 'Tiffin' dishes, often favoured by those visitors with more sensitive palates. Add to all this the unique nonya food, a style of cuisine created by the early settlers from China who adapted their old style of cooking to the available local produce and spices and it becomes obvious why Singapore, perhaps like nowhere else, is able to satisfy and delight even the most demanding gourmand.

I've kept in mind this diversity of culinary cultures when choosing the recipes and although limitation of space has made it impossible to include more than a cross section of what Singapore has to offer I believe it to be a fair and proportionate one. While most of the recipes came from professional chefs I have, in editing, made certain deliberate changes to allow for easier preparation in domestic kitchens. I've also followed certain other 'ground rules' and I hope that by offering a brief explanation of these the recipes will be easier to follow and provide you with results you'll be proud to serve up to family and friends alike.

*As this is a book of Asian recipes printed in English I have assumed that most readers will already have a more than average interest in cooking so I have generally avoided terms such as skinning, peeling, scaling, gutting and plucking and have, in most recipes, used the all-embracing 'clean and prepare'.

*At first glance some of the recipes may appear complicated but nearly always in Asian cooking more time is spent on the preparation rather than the cooking so with a little forward planning it's a simple matter to serve a multi-course meal with a minimum of fuss and delay.

*Meals in Asian homes usually consist of a number of dishes being served simultaneously so allowing each diner to select as personal preference dictates. There is usually a soup, two or three main courses, some vegetables and the ubiquitous bowl of rice. While a limited number of mouthwatering desserts are offered in many restaurants, a family meal (particularly so at a Chinese table) is most often concluded with fresh fruits. With this in mind, and assuming a family of four to six people, the quantities for the recipes were set. A specific number of servings, therefore, has not been indicated for individual recipes and if a western-style two-or-three course meal is being served, or if one or more recipe is being used as part of a larger overall meal, some quantity adjustments may be necessary.

*Singapore is justly renowned for its food stalls, where locals and visitors alike enjoy their favourite 'hawkers' food from early morning to late at night. These days, the less adventurous can enjoy this food in clinical air-conditioned coffee shops but I, like many others, believed it is that much better in authentic surroundings, and so I have placed some of the best known of these recipes in a separate section.

Recipes in this edition are written in standard American measures, having been converted from the original metric quantities. However, regardless of which system is followed it should be noted that Asian cooks tend to be less dependent on scales and measuring cups than many of their Western counterparts. In particular, where a recipe calls for the use of a number of spices the best results to suit personal tastes will only come after some 'trial and error'.

The 'wok' so often mentioned throughout the book is such a versatile utensil that I believe it deserves a pride of place in every kitchen regardless of the style of food being prepared. Having said that, however, I must add that heavy-based frying pans and saucepans should prove quite satisfactory for the following recipes.

*For the sake of simplicity I decided to title each recipe in English and to make each briefly descriptive rather than to provide an accurate translation from the ethnic original.

Soups

SPICY CHICKEN SOUP

1 medium size chicken
4 spring onions
1 brown onion
3/4 inch knob fresh ginger
2 stalks lemon grass
2 curry leaves
1 tsp salt
10 black peppercorns
6 shallots
3 cloves garlic
1/2 tsp blachan (shrimp paste)
3 Tbsp peanut oil
1 tsp coriander powder
1 tsp turmeric powder
2 Tbsp fresh lemon juice
2 Tbsp crispy fried onion

Joint the chicken, place in a large saucepan and cover with 2 quarts of cold water. Chop the spring onions, brown onion, ginger and lemon grass. Add these to the pan together with the curry leaves, salt and black peppercorns. Bring to the boil, then lower the heat, cover the pan and simmer until the chicken is tender, approximately 1 hour. Allow to cool, then remove the chicken, cut the meat from the bones and slice finely. Pour the stock through a fine strainer and set aside. Chop the shallots and crush the garlic and the blachan. Heat the oil in a clean saucepan and stir-fry the shallots until golden brown. Add the garlic and blachan and continue to stir over a moderate heat for 3 minutes. Add the coriander and turmeric powder, lemon juice and stock and bring to the boil. Lower the heat, cover the pan and simmer very slowly for 20 minutes, removing the lid and stirring occasionally. Finally, add the slices of chicken, adjust seasonings to taste and simmer, uncovered, for a further 5-10 minutes. To serve: pour into individual soup bowls and sprinkle the crispy fried onion on top.

CHICKEN LIVER & GINGER SOUP

7 oz chicken livers
3 oz chicken giblets
4 black Chinese mushrooms
3/4 inch knob of fresh ginger
1 spring onion
2 Tbsp peanut oil
2 Tbsp Chinese wine
salt to taste
freshly ground black pepper
fresh coriander leaves

Bring a pan of water to the boil, add the chicken liver and blanch, then remove, slice and set aside. Add the giblets and cook for 15 minutes, then discard the giblets and strain the stock through a fine sieve. Meanwhile, soak the mushrooms in warm water for 40 minutes, discard the hard stems and chop the caps. Slice the ginger and chop the spring onion. Heat the oil in a wok, add the ginger and stir-fry for 2-3 minutes. Then add the mushroom, liver and spring onion, and cook for a further minute. Pour in the stock and bring to the boil then add the wine and season to taste with salt and pepper. Lower the heat and allow to simmer for 10 minutes then transfer to a soup tureen and garnish with fresh coriander leaves.

Photo previous page: *Spicy Chicken Soup*

DUCK & YAM SOUP

1 young duck
4 carrots
4 tomatoes
4 brown onions
2 shallots
1 inch knob fresh ginger
4 cloves garlic
15 black peppercorns
1/2 tsp salt
4 oz preserved soya beans
1 1/4 lb yam
2 Tbsp vegetable oil

Prepare the duck and, with a sharp knife, remove most of the meat. Chop the meat into small pieces and place the carcass into a large stock pot. Chop coarsely the carrots, tomatoes, half the onions and shallots and shred half the ginger and garlic. Add these to the stock pot together with half the peppercorns and cover with 2 quarts of cold water. Bring to the boil, add 1 teaspoon of salt and boil rapidly for 2 minutes. Lower the heat, remove the scum from the surface and place a tightly fitting lid on the pot. Simmer gently for about 2½ hours, then pass through a fine sieve and allow to cool. Chop finely the remaining onions, shallots, ginger and garlic and pound together with the remaining peppercorns and the salted soya beans to form a smooth paste. Peel the yam and cut into 1/2 inch cubes. Heat the oil in a deep saucepan and stir-fry the pounded spice mixture for 5 minutes. Add the duck meat and the yam and pour in the prepared stock. Bring to the boil and adjust seasonings to taste. Cover the pan and lower the heat to simmer gently for a further 45-50 minutes.

PORK AND CRAB BALL SOUP

6 oz pork
3 oz white fish fillet
4 oz crabmeat
3 black Chinese mushrooms
3 oz bamboo shoot
1 large carrot
2 tsp fried garlic flakes
1 egg
salt to taste
freshly ground black pepper
2 quarts chicken stock
2 spring onions
1 Tbsp light soya sauce
1 tsp dark soya sauce
2 Tbsp crispy-fried onion

Pass the pork and fish through a fine grinder and flake the crabmeat. Soak the mushrooms in warm water for 40 minutes, then discard the hard stems. Shred the mushrooms, bamboo shoot and carrot and place in a mixing bowl, together with the pork, fish, crabmeat and garlic. Beat the egg lightly and add to the bowl, then season to taste with salt and pepper and mix to blend thoroughly. Shape the mixture into small balls and place in the refrigerator for 30 minutes. In a large pan bring the stock to a rapid boil and add the meatballs, spring onion and soya sauce. Boil rapidly for 3 minutes, then lower the heat and allow to simmer for a further 20 minutes. Finally, transfer to a soup tureen and sprinkle the crispy-fried onion on top.

SHARK'S FIN WITH CHICKEN

14 oz dried shark's fin
2 dried Chinese mushrooms
6 oz white chicken meat
3 oz ham
1/2 inch knob fresh ginger
2 spring onions
2 Tbsp peanut oil
1¼ quarts chicken stock
1 Tbsp Chinese wine
1 Tbsp light soya sauce
2 tsp dark soya sauce
freshly ground black pepper
2 tsp cornstarch

Soak the shark's fin in cold water overnight. Bring a large pan of water to the boil, add the shark's fin and cover. Allow to simmer for 3-4 hours, then rinse under cold running water for 10 minutes and set aside. Meanwhile, soak the mushrooms in warm water for 40 minutes, then discard the hard stems and slice the caps. Cut the chicken, ham and ginger into fine shreds and chop the onions. Pour the oil into a double boiler and place over a moderate heat. Add the ginger and onion and stir-fry for 2 minutes, then pour in the stock and bring to the boil. Add the shark's fin, mushroom, chicken, ham, wine, soya sauce and pepper and cover with a tightly fitting lid. Place over gently boiling water and cook for 1½ hours, then remove the shark's fin and transfer to individual soup bowls. Mix the cornstarch with a small quantity of cold water and stir into the stock. Bring back to a rapid boil and pour over the shark's fin. Serve immediately.

RAW FISH & VEGETABLE SOUP

14 oz white fish fillets
6 lettuce leaves
1/2 inch knob fresh ginger
1 small head broccoli
2 spring onions
oil for frying
1 tsp sesame oil
1 1/2 quarts fish stock
salt
freshly ground white pepper
fresh coriander leaves

Cut the fish into thin slices and ensure that no bones remain. Tear the lettuce leaves, cut the ginger into thin strips and chop the broccoli and spring onion. Heat the oil in a small pan and stir-fry the ginger and broccoli for 3-4 minutes, then remove and drain on kitchen paper. Place the lettuce leaves in the bottom of a soup tureen, add the fish, ginger, broccoli and spring onions and sprinkle the sesame oil on top. Bring the stock to the boil, season to taste with salt and pepper and pour over the fish. Garnish with fresh coriander and serve immediately.

SHREDDED BEEF & EGG SOUP

6 oz lean beef
$^{1}/_{4}$ tsp salt
$^{1}/_{4}$ tsp black pepper
1 tsp cornstarch
$^{1}/_{2}$ tsp baking soda
2 Tbsp peanut oil
1 Tbsp light soya sauce
1 tsp dark soya sauce
1 tsp sesame oil
$1^{1}/_{2}$ quarts chicken stock
2 egg whites
freshly chopped spring onion
freshly chopped coriander

Shred the beef and season with salt and freshly ground black pepper. Combine the cornstarch, baking soda, peanut oil and soya sauce, and pour over the beef. Sprinkle the sesame oil on top and allow to marinate for 20 minutes. Remove the beef and strain, retaining the marinade. In a large saucepan bring some water to the boil, add the beef and boil rapidly for 3 minutes, stirring continuously. Pour off the water and add the stock to the pan. Bring back to the boil and allow to simmer for 10 minutes, then pour in the reserved marinade and continue to simmer for a further 5 minutes. Beat the egg whites and gradually stir into the soup tureen and garnish with the chopped spring onions and coriander.

LENTIL SOUP

$^{3}/_{4}$ cup lentils
1 brown onion
2 tomatoes
2 Tbsp vegetable oil
$^{1}/_{2}$ tsp curry powder
$^{1}/_{2}$ tsp cumin powder
$1^{1}/_{2}$ quarts chicken stock
$^{1}/_{2}$ cup thin coconut milk
salt to taste
freshly ground black pepper
freshly chopped parsley

Soak the lentils for 4 hours, then drain thoroughly. Chop finely the onion and tomatoes. Heat the oil and stir-fry the onion until it becomes soft and transparent, then add the tomatoes and continue to cook for 3 minutes. Add the lentils, curry powder, cumin and stock and bring to the boil. Lower the heat and cook slowly for approximately 1 hour, then add the coconut milk and season to taste with salt and pepper. Stir well and cook for a further few minutes, then transfer to a soup tureen and sprinkle the freshly chopped parsley on top.

MULLIGATAWNY SOUP

2 brown onions
2 carrots
1 cooking apple
3 Tbsp butter
3 Tbsp all-purpose flour
3 Tbsp curry powder
1¹/₂ quarts chicken stock
2 bay leaves
2 sprigs parsley
2 sprigs thyme
2 Tbsp tomato paste
salt to taste
freshly ground white pepper
2 Tbsp mango chutney
¹/₂ cup cooked rice
¹/₃ cup fresh cream

Dice the onions, carrots and apple. Melt the butter in a large saucepan, add the onion and carrot and cook for 2-3 minutes until the onion becomes soft. Add the flour and curry powder and stir-fry over a moderate heat for 2 minutes, then pour in the stock, stir well and bring to the boil. Make a bouquet-garni of the bay leaves, parsley and thyme and add to the stock together with the tomato paste and diced apple. Season to taste with salt and freshly ground white pepper, cover the pan, lower the heat and simmer gently for 1 hour. Then, remove from the heat, discard the bouquet-garni and allow the soup to cool. Pour through a coarse sieve into a fresh saucepan, pressing the vegetables with a wooden spoon. Just prior to serving, return the soup to the stove and bring back to the boil. Chop the chutney into tiny pieces and add this to the pan together with the cooked rice. Stir well and let simmer for a further minute, then stir in the cream and immediately transfer to a soup tureen.

WON TON SOUP

24 won ton wrappers
6 oz shrimps
6 oz fresh pork
4 oz peeled water chestnuts
salt to taste
freshly ground white pepper
¹/₂ small Chinese cabbage
egg-wash
1¹/₂ quarts chicken stock
1 Tbsp Chinese wine
2 tsp dark soya sauce
1 tsp sesame oil
1 Tbsp chopped spring onion

Lay the won ton wrappers flat on a lightly greased board. Shell and de-vein the shrimps. Grind together the shrimps, pork and chestnuts and season the mixture with salt and pepper. Shred the cabbage. Spoon a quantity of the shrimp mixture onto each wrapper, then fold them into triangles, crlmp slightly and seal with egg-wash. Bring the stock to the boil in a large pan, add the wine, soya sauce and cabbage and boil rapidly for 2 minutes. Reduce the heat, transfer the won tons to the stock and simmer for 5-6 minutes, then transfer the won tons to the soup bowls. Adjust seasonings to taste and pour the stock into the bowls. Finally, sprinkle on the sesame oil and garnish with chopped spring onion.

Seafoods

CRAB IN BLACK BEAN SAUCE

1 large fresh crab
¼ tsp white pepper
1 egg white
2 Tbsp cornstarch
1 green pepper
1 brown onion
½ inch knob fresh ginger
1 clove garlic
1 Tbsp fermented black beans
oil for deep-frying
1 Tbsp Chinese wine
1 Tbsp light soya sauce
½ cup chicken stock
1 tsp sesame oil
1 tsp sugar

Steam the crab over rapidly boiling water for 15 minutes, then remove the top shell and separate the claws from the body. Crack the claws and cut the body of the crab into serving-size pieces, then place in a dish and season with pepper. Whisk the egg white with half the cornstarch and pour over the crab. Set aside for 20 minutes. Chop the green pepper and onion, slice the ginger and mince the garlic. Mash the black beans with 2 tsp of oil. Heat the remaining oil in a wok until it is very hot (almost smoking) and deep-fry the crab for 2 minutes. Add the green pepper and onion and cook for a further minute, then remove all the ingredients with a slotted spoon and drain on kitchen paper. Pour away most of the oil and replace the crab. Add the ginger and garlic and stir-fry for 2 minutes, then add the black beans and stir for a further minute. Add the wine, soya sauce, stock, sesame oil and sugar and bring to the boil. Mix the remaining cornstarch with a small quantity of cold water and stir into the sauce to thicken slightly, then transfer to serving dish.

CHILLI CRAB

3 large fresh crabs
6 fresh red chillies
¾ inch knob fresh ginger
2 cloves garlic
½ cup vegetable oil
2 Tbsp sugar
salt to taste
freshly ground black pepper
1¼ cups chicken stock
2 tsp vinegar
2 tsp light soya sauce
2 Tbsp tomato sauce
1 egg
chunks of white bread

Scrub the crabs with a stiff brush and rinse well under cold running water. Remove the claws and smash slightly. Chop the crab backs into medium size pieces taking care to discard the grey and pulpy matter. Chop the chillies, ginger and garlic. Heat the oil in a wok and cook the crabs for 1-2 minutes, stirring frequently, then remove the crabs to the side of the wok and pour off most of the oil. Add the chilli, ginger and garlic and stir-fry for 2-3 minutes, then return the crab to the heat, add the sugar, salt and freshly ground black pepper and pour in the stock. Stir well then bring to the boil, cover the pan and simmer slowly until the crab is cooked, approximately 15 minutes. Remove the cover and add the vinegar, soya sauce and tomato sauce. Beat the egg lightly, add this to the sauce and stir for a further minute until the egg begins to set and the sauce thickens slightly. Serve with chunks of white bread for eating with sauce.

Photo previous page: *Crab in Black Bean Sauce*

LOBSTER WITH PEPPERS

1 large fresh lobster
1 tsp cornstarch
1 small red pepper
1 small green pepper
1 inch knob fresh ginger
1 spring onion
1 clove garlic
1/2 cup peanut oil
2 tsp light soya sauce
1 Tbsp Chinese wine
1 tsp sugar
3/4 cup fish stock
salt
freshly ground black pepper
fresh coriander leaves

Place the lobster in a pan of rapidly boiling water and cook for 20-30 minutes, allowing 5-6 minutes per pound. Let cool, then remove the meat and cut into bite-size pieces. Sprinkle the cornstarch over the lobster meat and set aside for 15 minutes. Chop the red and green peppers, shred the ginger and spring onion and crush the garlic. Heat the oil in a wok and stir-fry the lobster for 2-3 minutes, then remove the meat and pour away most of the oil. Reheat the wok, add the ginger and garlic and stir-fry for 3 minutes, then add the peppers and spring onion and replace the lobster. Stir-fry for a further minute, then add the soya sauce, wine, sugar and stock and bring to the boil. Lower the heat and season to taste with salt and pepper. Continue to cook slowly for 3 minutes, then transfer to a serving dish and garnish with fresh coriander.

LOBSTER OMELETTE

1 fresh lobster
2 tsp vinegar
salt
freshly ground black pepper
1/2 inch knob fresh ginger
2 cloves garlic
2 spring onions
vegetable oil for frying
2 Tbsp light soya sauce
2 Tbsp Chinese wine
8 eggs
1 tsp sesame oil

Place the lobster in a large pan of rapidly boiling water, add the vinegar and cook for 15-20 minutes. Remove the meat from the shell, chop into bite size pieces and season with salt and pepper. Cut the ginger into fine shreds, crush the garlic and chop the spring onions. Heat a small quantity of vegetable oil in a wok and stir-fry the ginger and garlic for 3-4 minutes, then add the lobster, spring onion, soya sauce and Chinese wine. Stir over a moderate heat for 2 minutes, then transfer to a large bowl. Beat the eggs lightly and pour into the bowl, then add the sesame oil and mix thoroughly. Heat more vegetable oil in a clean wok and pour in the egg mixture. Cook over a fairly low heat until the egg sets, turning occasionally to break up the omelette. Transfer to a serving plate and serve immediately.

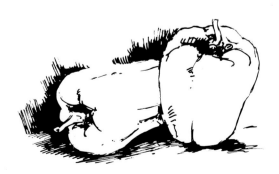

FRIED SHRIMPS IN SZECHUAN SAUCE

1 ¼ lbs jumbo shrimps
1 brown onion
1 red pepper
1 inch knob fresh ginger
3 cloves garlic
oil for deep frying
2 tsp chilli bean paste
1 Tbsp tomato sauce
1 Tbsp Chinese wine
½ cup chicken stock
2 tsp sugar
salt to taste
freshly ground white pepper
1 tsp cornstarch

Remove the heads and tails from the shrimps, but leave the shells intact. Cut in half and remove the black veins. Chop the onion, red pepper and ginger and crush the garlic. Heat the oil in a wok until it starts to smoke, then deep-fry the shrimps for 2 minutes. Remove the shrimps and drain on kitchen paper. Pour away most of the oil. Replace the wok over a moderate heat, add the onion, pepper, ginger and garlic and stir-fry for 2-3 minutes. Add the bean paste, tomato sauce, wine, stock, sugar, salt and pepper and bring to the boil. Replace the shrimps and cook over a moderate heat for a further 2 minutes, stirring frequently. Finally, mix the cornstarch with a small quantity of cold water and stir into the sauce to thicken slightly. Serve immediately.

CURRIED SHRIMPS

1¹/₂ lbs fresh medium size shrimps
2 shallots
4 fresh red chillies
³/₄ inch knob fresh ginger
2 cloves garlic
4 candlenuts
³/₄ tsp coriander seeds
³/₄ tsp cumin seeds
1 tsp turmeric powder
¹/₂ tsp salt
4 Tbsp vegetable oil
2¹/₂ cups thick coconut milk
freshly chopped coriander leaves

Shell and de-vein the shrimps leaving the tails intact. Chop the shallots, chillies, ginger and garlic and grind together with the candlenuts, coriander, cumin, turmeric and salt. Add 1 Tbsp of oil to produce a smooth paste. Heat the remaining oil in a wok and stir-fry the spice-paste for 3-4 minutes, then add one third of the coconut milk and bring to the boil. Stir over a moderately hot heat for a further minute, then add the shrimps and half the remaining coconut milk. Bring back to the boil, then lower heat and allow to simmer for 5-6 minutes. Finally, add the remaining coconut milk, bring to a rapid boil and cook until the sauce has reduced by half. Transfer to a serving dish and sprinkle the freshly chopped coriander on top.

CHILLI SHRIMPS WITH GINGER

1¼ lb fresh shrimps
salt
freshly ground black pepper
3 Tbsp Chinese wine
1 egg white
1 Tbsp cornstarch
6 fresh red chillies
1 inch knob fresh ginger
2 cloves garlic
oil for deep frying
2 Tbsp light soya sauce
1 Tbsp vinegar
1 Tbsp sugar

Shell and de-vein the shrimps and place in a shallow dish. Season with salt and pepper and sprinkle with half the wine. Set aside for 20 minutes. Beat the egg white with the cornstarch and pour over the shrimps, tossing well to ensure an even coating. Chop the chillies and ginger and crush the garlic. Heat the oil in a wok until it starts to smoke and deep-fry the shrimps until golden, then remove, drain thoroughly and set aside. Pour off most of the oil, re-heat the wok and add the chilli, ginger and garlic. Stir-fry over a fairly high heat for 3-4 minutes, then add the soya sauce, vinegar, sugar and remaining wine and bring to the boil. Stir well, then lower the heat, replace the shrimps and cook for a further 45 seconds.

SWEET & SOUR SHRIMPS

1½ lbs fresh shrimps
1 egg
3 Tbsp vinegar
1 Tbsp Chinese wine
1 Tbsp light soya sauce
1 Tbsp tomato sauce
2 tsp sugar
¼ tsp salt
¼ tsp black pepper
2 Tbsp cornstarch
1 large brown onion
1 green pepper
2 spring onions
2 fresh red chillies
¾ inch knob fresh ginger
⅓ cup vegetable oil
½ cup canned pineapple chunks

Shell and de-vein the shrimps, rinse under cold running water and place in a shallow dish. Beat the egg lightly, mix with the vinegar, Chinese wine, soya sauce, tomato sauce, sugar, salt and pepper and pour over the shrimps. Allow to stand for 15 minutes, then remove shrimps and dust with the cornstarch. Retain the marinade. Slice the brown onion, cut the pepper into medium size pieces and finely chop the spring onions, chillies and ginger. Heat the oil in a wok and stir-fry the shrimps for 2-3 minutes, then remove and set aside. Pour away half the oil from the wok, then add the onion and stir-fry until it starts to brown. Next, add the green pepper, spring onion, chilli and ginger and retain over a fairly high heat for 3-4 minutes, stirring frequently. Finally, replace the shrimps add the pineapple chunks and reserved marinade and adjust seasonings to taste. Stir well and allow to simmer for a further minute before transferring to a serving dish.

CUTTLEFISH IN OYSTER SAUCE

1 lb small cuttlefish
3 Tbsp vegetable oil
2 shallots
2 fresh red chillies
1/2 inch knob fresh ginger
2 cloves garlic
1/3 cup oyster sauce
1 Tbsp light soya sauce
1 tsp dark soya sauce
2 Tbsp Chinese wine
1 tsp vinegar
1 tsp sugar
freshly ground black pepper
1 tsp sesame oil

Discard the head section and ink sac and wash the cuttlefish under cold running water, boil in lightly salted water for 2 minutes, then drain and set aside. Heat the oil in a wok over a moderate heat. Chop finely the shallots, chillies, ginger and garlic, add to the wok and stir-fry for 1 minute, then add the cuttlefish and continue to cook for a further minute, stirring frequently. Then pour away most of oil and add the oyster sauce, soya sauce, wine, vinegar, sugar and pepper. Bring to the boil, stir in the sesame oil and transfer to a serving dish.

DEEP FRIED CUTTLEFISH

1 1/4 lb cuttlefish
3 fresh red chillies
2 cloves garlic
1 tsp baking soda
vegetable oil for deep frying
2 Tbsp peanut oil
2 tsp sugar
3 Tbsp tomato sauce
1 Tbsp Worcestershire sauce
salt to taste
freshly ground black pepper
lettuce leaves
2 tsp finely chopped parsley

Clean the cuttlefish and remove the head, tentacles and backbone. Cut the chillies into julienne strips and crush the garlic. Bring a pan of water to the boil, add the baking soda and boil the cuttlefish for 10 minutes, then pour into a colander, drain and pat dry with a paper towel. Heat the vegetable oil in a wok until it is smoking and deep-fry the cuttlefish for 2-3 minutes until the outside skin is crispy, then remove and drain off all excess oil. Clean the wok and heat the peanut oil, then add the chilli and garlic and stir-fry for 3 minutes. Add the sugar, tomato sauce, Worcestershire sauce, salt and freshly ground pepper and stir to blend thoroughly. Finally, return the cuttlefish and cook for a further minute, stirring frequently. To serve; arrange crispy lettuce leaves on a serving plate, place the cuttlefish on top and garnish with finely chopped parsley.

SPICY FRIED COCKLES

1¼ lb cockles or clams
4 fresh red chillies
4 cloves garlic
3 Tbsp peanut oil
1 Tbsp tomato sauce
2 tsp dark soya sauce
2 tsp black bean sauce
salt to taste
freshly ground black pepper
2 tsp cornstarch
2 tsp fresh lime juice

Wash the cockles, then place for 2 minutes in boiling water. Remove from the shells. Chop the chillies and crush the garlic. Heat the oil until very hot, add the chilli and garlic and stir-fry for 3 minutes, stirring frequently, then add the tomato sauce, soya sauce, black bean sauce and ½ cup of cold water. Bring to the boil, then lower heat, season to taste with salt and pepper and allow to simmer for a further 3 minutes. Finally, mix the cornstarch with a small quantity of cold water and stir into the sauce to thicken slightly. Transfer to a serving dish and sprinkle the lime juice on top.

CLAMS IN SPICY SAUCE

1 lb small clams
1 brown onion
2 shallots
¾ inch knob fresh ginger
2 fresh green chillies
2 cloves garlic
2 Tbsp peanut oil
3 Tbsp tomato sauce
1 tsp sugar
2½ cups clear fish stock
salt to taste
freshly ground white pepper
2 tsp cornstarch

Scrub the clams with a hard brush and rinse under running water. Finely chop the brown onion, shallots, ginger and chillies and crush the garlic. Heat the oil in a pan and stir-fry the chopped vegetables for 3 minutes. Add the tomato sauce, sugar and fish stock. Bring to the boil and season to taste with salt and freshly ground pepper. Add the clams, lower heat and simmer until the clams open, approximately 3-4 minutes. Place the clams in a serving dish. Mix the cornstarch with a small quantity of cold water, stir into the sauce and allow to thicken slightly then pour over the clams.

Photo opposite page: *Spicy Fried Cockles & Clams in Spicy Sauce*

SEAFOOD STEAMBOAT

12 mussels
12 fishballs (see below)
12 medium-size shrimps
1 small lobster
8 oz cuttlefish
10 oz garoupa fillets
10 oz red snapper fillets
leaf vegetables (spinach, lettuce,
Chinese cabbage)
clear stock for cooking
2 Tbsp Chinese wine
1 tsp finely chopped ginger
1 tsp finely chopped red chilli
1 tsp dark soya sauce
1/2 tsp sesame oil
salt to taste
freshly ground black pepper

Dip:
1 shallot
2 fresh red chillies
1/2 inch knob fresh ginger
1 clove garlic
1 tsp sugar
1 Tbsp fresh lime juice
2 Tbsp light soya sauce
2 Tbsp stock

Fishballs:
5 oz wolf herring fillets
2 tsp cornstarch
salt to taste
freshly ground black pepper

Clean and prepare the seafood and vegetables. Place the mussels in a pan together with the stock and 1 Tbsp of wine and cover with a tightly fitting lid. Cook over a moderate heat, shaking the pan occasionally, until the shells open, discarding any that fail to do so. Cook the fishballs in rapidly boiling salted water for 5 minutes, then remove and drain. Shell and de-vein the shrimps, cut along the back and fold open. Remove the meat from the lobster and cut into chunks. Cut the cuttlefish, garoupa and snapper into large bite-size pieces. Arrange the seafood on a large serving plate and place on the table next to a steamboat (kettle and stove). Pour the stock into the steamboat, add the ginger and chilli and bring to the boil. Season with soya sauce, sesame oil, remaining wine, salt and pepper and add the vegetables. Reduce the heat slightly and cook for 2-3 minutes, then place pieces of seafood into small wire baskets and cook in the stock. (The heat should be continually adjusted to keep the stock at a gentle simmer). Serve with the prepared dip.

To make the dip: chop the shallot, chillies, ginger and garlic into very tiny dice and mix with the sugar, lime juice, soya sauce and stock.

To make the fishballs: place the fish through a coarse grinder and mix with the cornstarch and a small quantity of cold water. Season to taste with salt and pepper and roll into small balls. Dip in iced-water and refrigerate for 1 hour before cooking.

Photo opposite page: *Seafood Steamboat*

FRIED STUFFED MACKEREL

4 mackerel
1 tsp salt
1/2 tsp white pepper
1 brown onion
3 fresh red chillies
1 inch knob fresh ginger
2 cloves garlic
2 stalks lemon grass
6 oz dried shrimps
3 oz blachan (shrimp paste)
2 Tbsp tomato sauce
2 tsp dark soya sauce
oil for frying
cucumber wedges
onion rings

Clean and prepare the fish. Slit lengthways and carefully remove the backbones, then season with salt and pepper. Chop the onion, chillies, ginger, garlic and lemon grass and place in a mortar. Add the shrimps, blachan, tomato sauce and soya sauce and pound thoroughly, then stuff the mixture into the fish. Heat the oil until it starts to smoke and fry the fish, then transfer to a serving plate and garnish with cucumber wedges and onion rings.

DEEP-FRIED FISH FILLETS

1 lb garoupa fillets
1 tsp salt
1/2 tsp white pepper
2 spring onions
1/2 inch knob fresh ginger
4 Tbsp Chinese wine
1 tsp sesame oil
1 tsp sugar
2 eggs
1 cup all-purpose flour
1/2 tsp baking soda
oil for deep-frying

Cut the fillets into serving-size pieces, place in a shallow dish and season with salt and pepper. Chop finely the spring onions and ginger and mix with the wine, sesame oil and sugar. Stir until the sugar is dissolved, then pour over the fish and set aside for 30 minutes. Break the eggs into a mixing bowl and whisk lightly, then add the flour, baking soda and sufficient cold water to make a smooth thin batter. Remove the fish from the marinade and drain on kitchen paper, then coat with the batter. Heat the oil until it is very hot, then reduce the heat and add the fish. Deep-fry until the fish is cooked and the outside is golden and crispy.

STEAMED FISH WITH GINGER

1 whole white fish, approx 1 1/2 lb
1/2 tsp salt
1/4 tsp black pepper
3/4 inch knob fresh ginger
3 spring onions
3 Tbsp light soya sauce
2 Tbsp peanut oil

Clean and scale the fish but do not remove the head or tail. With a sharp knife, make an incision along the underside and remove the backbone. Season the fish with the salt and pepper and set aside for 30 minutes. Chop the ginger and spring onions very finely, mix with the soya sauce and stuff into the prepared pocket of the fish. Place on a steamer rack. Heat the peanut oil and pour over the fish, then place the rack over boiling water, cover and cook for approximately 20 minutes.

STIR-FRIED FISH & VEGETABLES

1 lb white fish fillets
¼ tsp salt
¼ tsp black pepper
1 egg white
1 Tbsp cornstarch
1 tsp sesame oil
2 spring onions
2 cloves garlic
½ inch knob fresh ginger
4 oz button mushrooms
4 oz baby corn
¾ cup green peas
2 Tbsp peanut oil
1 cup chicken stock
2 tsp light soya sauce
1 tsp sugar
1 tsp Chinese wine

Cut the fish into bite-size pieces taking care to remove any remaining small bones. Place in a shallow dish and season with salt and pepper. Whisk the egg white with half the cornstarch until smooth, then stir in the sesame oil and pour over the fish. Finely chop the spring onions, garlic and ginger and prepare the vegetables. Heat half the peanut oil in a wok, add the vegetables and stir-fry for 2 minutes, then add the stock, soya sauce and sugar and bring to the boil. Cook for a further minute, then remove the vegetables, drain and set aside. Reserve the stock. Clean the wok and heat the remaining oil. Add the onion, garlic and ginger and stir-fry over a moderate heat for 1 minute, then add the fish and continue to cook for 2 minutes, stirring frequently. Replace the vegetables and adjust seasonings to taste, then pour in the reserved sauce and bring to the boil. Mix the remaining cornstarch with a small quantity of cold water and stir in to the sauce. Cook for a further 30 seconds, stir in the wine, then transfer to a serving dish.

FRIED FISH CURRY

1¼ lb pomfret fillets
½ tsp chilli powder
½ tsp English mustard powder
½ tsp salt
¼ tsp white pepper
3 Tbsp fresh lime juice
¾ cup all-purpose flour
4 shallots
1 inch knob fresh ginger
2 fresh red chillies
1 fresh green chilli
2 cloves garlic
½ cup ghee
1 tsp curry powder
1 cup thick coconut milk

Remove any skin from the fish, cut the fillets into bite-size pieces and place in a shallow dish. Sprinkle the chilli powder, mustard, salt and white pepper over the fish and pour the lime juice on top. Set aside for 20 minutes, then coat the marinated fish with the flour. Chop the shallots, ginger and chilli and crush the garlic. Heat two thirds of the ghee in a pan and fry the pieces of fish until they are golden brown, then remove from the pan and drain. Clean the pan, add the remaining ghee and place over a high heat. When the ghee is very hot, add the shallot, ginger and garlic and stir-fry for 3-4 minutes, then add the green chilli, curry powder and coconut milk and bring to the boil. Finally, replace the fish, lower heat, and simmer gently for 5-6 minutes.

STEAMED POMFRET ROLLS

1 pomfret
½ tsp salt
¼ tsp white pepper
1 Tbsp Chinese wine
4 oz cooked ham
1 inch knob fresh ginger
3 spring onions
2 tsp peanut oil
freshly chopped coriander leaves

Scale and clean the fish. Carefully remove the fillets and extract all the small bones but leave the backbone, head and tail intact. Slice the fillets into 2 inch lengths and flatten slightly with the side of a knife. Season with salt and pepper and sprinkle the wine on top, then set aside for 20 minutes. Cut the ham, ginger and spring onions into thin strips. Place one strip each of ham, ginger and onion on top of each fish fillet and roll up, leaving a little stuffing showing at both ends. When all the rolls have been made arrange them on the carcass of the pomfret and place in a steamer. Sprinkle the peanut oil over the fish and cook for 8-10 minutes. Finally, transfer to a serving plate and garnish with the freshly chopped coriander.

FISH IN WINE SAUCE

6 fillets of white fish
¹/₂ tsp salt
¹/₄ tsp white pepper
1 egg white
1 tsp dark soya sauce
1 Tbsp cornstarch
3 oz dried fungus
(wood-ear mushrooms)
oil for deep-frying
2 Tbsp Chinese wine
¹/₂ cup clear fish stock
2 tsp sugar

Lay the fish fillets in a shallow dish and season with salt and pepper. Whisk together the egg white, soya sauce and half the cornstarch, pour over the fish and set aside for 20 minutes. Soak the fungus in warm water for 30 minutes, then rinse well under cold running water. Heat the oil in a wok until it is very hot (almost smoking), add the fish and fry for 30 seconds, then remove and drain on kitchen paper. Pour off most of the oil from the wok, then add the fungus and stir-fry for 2 minutes. Add the wine, stock and sugar, bring to the boil and adjust seasonings to taste. Mix the remaining cornstarch with a small quantity of cold water and stir into the sauce to thicken slightly, then replace the fish, cook for 1 minute and serve.

Poultry

SPICY STEAMED CHICKEN

1 young chicken
2 Tbsp chilli powder
1 Tbsp coriander powder
1 Tbsp cumin powder
1 Tbsp garam masala
1 tsp salt
1/2 tsp black pepper
2/3 cup fresh lime juice
oil for deep frying

Clean and prepare the chicken and place in a shallow dish. Mix together the spices, salt, pepper and lime juice and pour over the chicken. Place in the refrigerator and leave to marinate for 4 hours, turning occasionally. Then, remove and pat dry with kitchen paper. Heat the oil in a large pan and deep-fry the chicken until the skin is golden brown and crispy. Drain off all the excess oil and then place the chicken on a rack inside a large pan containing a small quantity of water. Place over a high heat and bring to the boil, then cover the pan with a tightly fitting lid, lower the heat and cook until the chicken is tender, approximately 40 minutes.

TANDOORI CHICKEN

2 small chickens
3 cloves garlic
2 fresh red chillies
3/4 inch knob fresh ginger
1/2 tsp salt
1/4 tsp saffron powder
2 Tbsp fresh lemon juice
1 cup natural yoghurt
2 tsp coriander powder
1 tsp cumin powder
1/4 tsp anise powder
1/4 tsp cayenne pepper
1 tsp paprika
1/3 cup ghee

Clean and prepare the chickens and remove the skin. Make sure the chickens are dried thoroughly, then, with a sharp knife, make slits in the thighs and breasts. Chop the garlic, chilli and ginger and pound together with the salt, saffron powder and lemon juice to form a smooth paste. Rub this paste into the flesh of the chickens and put them to one side for 30 minutes. In the meantime, mix the yoghurt with the coriander, cumin, anise, cayenne pepper, paprika and any remaining spice-paste. Arrange the chickens in a casserole dish, add the yoghurt mixture and place in a refrigerator to marinate for at least 12 hours. After removing from the marinade, baste the chickens with ghee, place on a rotisserie and cook in a moderately hot oven for 15-20 minutes. Then, lower the heat slightly, baste again with ghee and continue to cook until the chickens are tender. Serve with naan (a flat Indian bread) and an onion and tomato salad.

Note: In professional kitchens a special clay oven, known as a tandoori, is used for cooking this dish. The oven, heated by hot coals, opens at the bottom and provides a distinctive flavour that is hard to match at home. However, don't despair. Cooking in a charcoal oven is the next best thing but even without this, if the chicken is tender and well marinated, the results should prove highly satisfying.

Photo previous page: *Spicy Steamed Chicken*

PAPER-WRAPPED CHICKEN

1¼ lbs chicken meat
3 oz chicken livers
¾ inch knob fresh ginger
2 spring onions
1 clove garlic
2 Tbsp Chinese wine
2 Tbsp light soya sauce
2 Tbsp oyster sauce
1 tsp sesame oil
1 tsp sugar
1 Tbsp cornstarch
salt to taste
freshly ground white pepper
oil for deep-frying

Prepare and de-bone the chicken and cut into bite-size pieces. Cut the liver into thin slices. Chop the ginger and spring onions and crush the garlic. Place all the above in a shallow dish and add the Chinese wine, soya sauce, oyster sauce, sesame oil, sugar, cornstarch, salt and pepper. Set in the refrigerator and allow to marinate for 1 hour, occasionally turning the pieces of chicken. Cut out squares of greaseproof paper and place a piece of chicken in the centre of each. Wrap up like an envelope, folding in the end flap to secure completely. Heat the oil in a wok and when it begins to smoke, add the chicken-parcels and deep-fry for 4-5 minutes, stirring frequently with a slotted spoon. To serve: drain off excess oil and transfer to a serving plate (the chicken should remain wrapped until the last minute before eating).

CHICKEN WITH DRIED CHILLIES

1 lb chicken meat
½ tsp salt
½ tsp white pepper
2 Tbsp cornstarch
6 dried red chillies
3 spring onions
2 cloves garlic
1 inch knob fresh ginger
10 black peppercorns
½ cup peanut oil
1 Tbsp light soya sauce
1 tsp dark soya sauce
1 tsp vinegar
3 Tbsp sugar
¼ tsp anise powder
2 Tbsp Chinese wine
1 tsp sesame oil

Cut the chicken into small bite-size pieces, place in a shallow dish and season with salt and pepper. Mix half the cornstarch with 2 Tbsp of cold water and pour over the chicken. Set aside for 20 minutes. Discard the stalks and seeds from the chillies and cut into short lengths, approximately 1 inch. Chop the onions, garlic and ginger and crush the peppercorns. Heat 2 Tbsp of oil in a wok and stir-fry the chicken for 1 minute, then remove and drain on kitchen paper. Heat the remaining oil, add the chillies and stir over a high heat until they start to blacken, then lower heat and add the onion, garlic and ginger. Cook for 1 minute, then replace the chicken, add the soya sauce, vinegar, sugar and anise powder and continue to cook over a moderate heat for a further 2-3 minutes, stirring frequently. Finally, add the wine and sesame oil, stir well and transfer to a serving dish.

PINEAPPLE CHICKEN

2 fresh pineapples
2 lbs chicken meat
salt
freshly ground black pepper
2 tsp cornstarch
1 brown onion
1 small red pepper
1/3 cup vegetable oil
2 tsp dark soya sauce
2 tsp light soya sauce
1 Tbsp Chinese wine
2/3 cup chicken stock
1 1/2 cups cooked rice
1 Tbsp slivered almonds

Cut the pineapples in half, lengthwise and scoop out the fruit. Cut into small cubes and set aside. Place the pineapple shells in a very low oven. Cut the chicken meat into slightly larger cubes, season with salt and pepper and dust with the cornstarch. Chop the onion and red pepper. Heat two-thirds of the oil in a pan and saute the chicken for 2 minutes, then add the soya sauce, wine and stock and replace the chicken. Bring to the boil, adjust seasonings to taste and continue to cook over a moderate heat for a further 3 minutes, then add the pineapple and stir to mix thoroughly. Heat the remaining oil in a clean pan, add the rice and stir until heated through. To serve: place a layer of rice in the bottom of each pineapple shell, add the chicken mixture and top with the slivered almonds.

STIR FRIED CHICKEN WITH CELERY

10 oz chicken breasts
1/2 tsp salt
1/4 tsp black pepper
1 Tbsp Chinese wine
2 dried Chinese mushrooms
4 sticks celery
2 shallots
3/4 inch knob fresh ginger
1 clove garlic
1/3 cup oil
1 Tbsp light soya sauce
2 tsp dark soya sauce
1 tsp sugar
1/3 cup chicken stock
1 tsp cornstarch

Slice the chicken, season with salt and pepper and sprinkle with the wine. Set aside for 30 minutes. Meanwhile, soak the mushrooms in warm water for 40 minutes, then remove the hard stems and slice the caps. Cut the celery into 1¼ inch lengths, slice the shallots and ginger and crush the garlic. Heat the oil in a wok, add the chicken and stir-fry for 2-3 minutes, then remove and drain. Re-heat the remaining oil in the wok, add the shallot, ginger and garlic and stir-fry for 3 minutes, then add the soya sauce, sugar and stock and bring to the boil. Add the mushrooms and celery and cook for 2 minutes, then replace the chicken and cook for a further 2-3 minutes. Finally, mix the cornstarch with a small quantity of cold water and stir into the sauce.

CHICKEN & CASHEWS WITH YAM

1 lb chicken meat
3/4 inch knob fresh ginger
2 fresh red chillies
1/4 tsp baking powder
2 Tbsp Chinese wine
1 Tbsp light soya sauce
salt
freshly ground black pepper
14 oz yam
2 tsp sugar
oil for deep frying
3 oz cashew nuts
finely chopped coriander leaves

Cut the chicken into small pieces and chop finely the ginger and chillies. Place the chicken, ginger and chillies in a dish, add the baking powder, Chinese wine, soya sauce, salt and freshly ground black pepper and set aside for 15 minutes. Peel the yam, cut into small cubes and cook in a double boiler over rapidly boiling water until soft, then add the sugar and mash with a wooden spoon. Roll out and shape into a ring approximately 8 inches in diameter, then place onto a rack and set aside. Next, heat a small quantity of the oil in a wok, add the chicken and all the marinade and stir-fry for 3-4 minutes. Add the cashew nuts and continue to cook over medium heat, stirring frequently, until the chicken is tender, then remove and set aside. Add the remaining oil to the wok, bring to the boil and deep-fry the yam ring for a few minutes, until it is golden and crispy. Then, remove, drain off excess oil and place on a serving dish. Fill the centre of the ring with the chicken and cashews and garnish with the coriander.

DRY CHICKEN CURRY

1 whole chicken
3 Tbsp curry powder
2 large brown onions
2 shallots
2 fresh red chillies
1 inch knob fresh ginger
2 cloves garlic
2 stalks lemon grass
1/3 cup thick coconut milk
2 Tbsp vegetable oil
1 tsp chilli powder
1 tsp turmeric powder
freshly ground white pepper
salt to taste
3/4 cup thin coconut milk

Clean and prepare the chicken, remove the skin and cut into serving size pieces. Coat the chicken with curry powder and set aside. Chop the onions, shallots, chillies, ginger, garlic and lemon grass. In a large saucepan bring the thick coconut milk to the boil and boil rapidly until the liquid has nearly all evaporated leaving an oily substance at the bottom of the pan. Add to this the vegetable oil and reheat. Add the onion, shallot and garlic and stir-fry for 3 minutes then add the chillies, ginger, lemon grass, chilli powder, turmeric powder, freshly ground white pepper and salt. Stir to blend thoroughly then add the pieces of chicken and pour in the thin coconut milk. Bring almost to boiling point and cook until the chicken is tender and most of the liquid has evaporated. Serve with steamed rice and 'tiffin' side dishes such as grated coconut, chopped peanuts, diced pineapple and tomato and mango chutney.

PIGEONS BAKED IN SALT

2 plump pigeons
4 shallots
4 spring onions
3/4 inch knob fresh ginger
1 clove garlic
3 Tbsp Chinese wine
2 Tbsp light soya sauce
2 tsp dark soya sauce
1/2 tsp anise powder
salt
freshly ground white pepper
2 1/4 lb rock salt

Clean and prepare the pigeons. Chop finely the shallots, spring onions, ginger and garlic and mix with the Chinese wine, soya sauce, anise powder, salt and pepper. Rub the mixture over the outside of the pigeons and stuff the remainder inside. Set aside for 1 hour, then wrap the birds individually in sheets of well-greased mulberry paper. Heat the rock salt in a wok until it is extremely hot, then bury the birds in the salt, place a cover on the wok and leave on a low heat for 10-12 minutes. Remove the birds and reheat the salt, then repeat the cooking process for a further 10 minutes. To serve: unwrap the pigeons, remove the stuffing, and chop the meat into bite-size pieces.

MINCED PIGEON WITH LETTUCE

2 plump pigeons
4 dried Chinese mushrooms
3 oz bamboo shoots
3 spring onions
1 inch knob fresh ginger
3 oz chicken livers
2 eggs
1 Tbsp cornstarch
2 Tbsp light soya sauce
2 tsp dark soya sauce
1 tsp sugar
1/2 tsp salt
1/4 tsp black pepper
4 Tbsp peanut oil
2 Tbsp Chinese wine
2 tsp oyster sauce
lettuce leaves
sweet plum sauce

Prepare the pigeons and boil until tender (approximately 30 minutes), then de-bone and mince the meat. Soak the mushrooms in warm water for 40 minutes, then remove and discard the hard stems. Finely chop the mushrooms, bamboo shoots, spring onions, ginger and chicken liver. Beat the eggs in a large bowl and add the cornstarch, soya sauce, sugar, salt and pepper. Place the minced pigeon and chopped chicken liver in the bowl and allow to stand for 20 minutes. Heat the oil in a wok, add the meat and stir-fry for 2-3 minutes. Remove and drain. Place the mushrooms, bamboo shoots, onion and ginger into the wok and stir for 2 minutes, then replace the meat, add the Chinese wine, oyster sauce and marinade and stir over medium heat for a further 3 minutes. Adjust seasonings to taste and, if necessary, thicken with a little extra cornstarch mixed with cold water. Transfer to a serving dish and place on the table together with a plate of lettuce leaves and a dish of plum sauce.

Note: Traditionally, this dish is eaten with the hands, each diner spooning a little meat onto a lettuce leaf, adding some sauce and rolling up the leaf.

Photo following page: *Minced Pigeon with Lettuce*

SMOKED DUCK

1 fat duck
1 tsp Chinese five-spice powder
1 tsp sugar
1/2 tsp salt
1/4 tsp white pepper
2 Tbsp honey
1 tsp fresh lemon juice

Sauce:
1/3 cup chilli sauce
2 tsp dark soya sauce
1/2 tsp freshly grated ginger
1/2 tsp crushed garlic
2 tsp sugar

Prepare the duck, clean thoroughly and secure the wings in order that they will not open during cooking. Mix the Chinese five-spice powder, sugar, salt and white pepper and rub the mixture inside the duck. In a saucepan bring 1/2 cup of water to the boil, add the honey and lemon juice and stir until the honey has completely dissolved. Allow the syrup to cool slightly, then rub all over the outside of the duck. Tie a string around the duck's neck and hang in a warm and draughty place to dry. Preferably the duck should then be cooked in a charcoal oven but if this is not available, place on a spit and cook over an open charcoal fire, turning frequently. Serve with a side dish of spiced sauce made by mixing together the chilli sauce, soya sauce, freshly grated ginger, crushed garlic and sugar.

DUCK IN LEMON SAUCE

4 breasts of duck
2 shallots
3/4 inch knob fresh ginger
4 egg yolks
2 Tbsp light soya sauce
3 Tbsp cornstarch
oil for deep frying
freshly sliced lemon

Sauce:
2 Tbsp butter
2 Tbsp rice flour
1/2 cup fresh lemon juice
1/2 cup chicken stock
2 Tbsp Chinese wine
1 Tbsp sugar
salt to taste
freshly ground black pepper
2 tsp cornstarch

De-bone the duck breasts and remove any skin. Slice the meat into bite-size pieces and place in a shallow dish. Chop the shallots and ginger very finely. Lightly beat the egg yolks in a bowl, add the shallot, ginger, soya sauce and 1 Tbsp of cornstarch and mix well. Pour the mixture over the duck and set aside in a cool place for 1 hour. Heat the oil in a wok until it starts to smoke. Coat the duck with the remaining cornstarch and deep-fry until tender and crispy. Remove the duck from the oil, drain thoroughly and arrange on a serving plate. Pour the hot sauce over the duck and garnish with lemon slices.

To make the sauce: melt the butter in a saucepan over a moderate heat, add the flour and blend thoroughly. Add the lemon juice and stock and bring to the boil, then add the wine, sugar, salt and pepper and stir for 1 minute. Finally, mix the cornstarch with a small quantity of cold water and stir into the sauce to thicken slightly.

Photo opposite page: *Duck in Lemon Sauce*

43

SWEET & SOUR PORK

1 lb pork tenderloin
¹/₂ tsp salt
¹/₄ tsp white pepper
¹/₄ tsp Chinese five-spice powder
2 eggs
2 Tbsp Chinese wine
2 Tbsp light soya sauce
1 tsp dark soya sauce
2 Tbsp cornstarch
oil for deep frying

Sauce:
1 brown onion
1 green pepper
1 large tomato
2 carrots
2 inch length cucumber
3 fresh red chillies
³/₄ inch knob fresh ginger
1 clove garlic
1 Tbsp vegetable oil
1 cup chicken stock
2 Tbsp Chinese wine
2 Tbsp light soya sauce
2 tsp dark soya sauce
2 tsp vinegar
2 Tbsp fresh lemon juice
3 Tbsp sugar
¹/₂ cup canned pineapple chunks
2 tsp cornstarch

Cut the pork into bite-size pieces and season with salt, white pepper and five-spice powder. Beat the eggs lightly, mix with the Chinese wine and soya sauce and pour over the pork. Allow the meat to marinate for 30 minutes, then remove and dust with cornstarch. Heat the oil in a wok until it starts to smoke, then add the pork, lower the heat and deep-fry for 4-5 minutes until it is well cooked and the outside is golden and crispy. Remove the meat, drain off excess oil and arrange on a serving dish. Pour the prepared sauce on top and serve immediately.

To make the sauce: chop the onion, green pepper and tomato coarsely, slice the carrots and cucumber, cut the chillies and ginger into julienne strips and crush the garlic. Place wok over a high heat, add the oil and stir-fry the vegetables for 2 minutes, then add the stock, Chinese wine, soya sauce, vinegar, lemon juice and sugar and bring to the boil. Lower the heat, add the pineapple chunks and continue to cook for a further 3 minutes, stirring frequently. Finally, mix the cornstarch with a small quantity of cold water and stir into the sauce to thicken slightly. Pour over the pork immediately.

PORK BALLS WITH CABBAGE

14 oz lean pork
¹/₂ tsp salt
¹/₄ tsp white pepper
1 tsp dark soya sauce
2 eggs
1 Tbsp cornstarch
1 small head Chinese cabbage
3 Tbsp vegetable oil
²/₃ cup chicken stock

Grind the pork and season with salt, pepper and soya sauce. Break the egg into a bowl and whisk lightly with half the cornstarch. Add the pork and mix well, then divide and shape into small balls. Chop the cabbage. Heat the oil in a wok, add the pork balls and stir over a moderate heat until well cooked and golden, then remove and drain on kitchen paper. Add the cabbage and stir-fry for 2-3 minutes, then pour in the stock and bring to the boil. Replace the meat, adjust seasonings to taste and allow to simmer until the stock has reduced by half, then transfer the pork and cabbage to a serving dish. Mix the remaining cornstarch with a small quantity of cold water and stir into the remaining stock to thicken slightly, then pour onto the pork and serve immediately.

OVEN-SMOKED SPARERIBS

2 lb ribs of pork
2 fresh red chillies
3/4 inch fresh ginger
2 cloves garlic
3 oz preserved beancurd
2 Tbsp light soya sauce
2 Tbsp sweet and sour sauce
2 Tbsp sugar
1/2 tsp salt
1/4 tsp white pepper
1/3 cup chilli sauce

Place the pork in a large shallow dish with the fat side facing upwards. Chop the chillies, ginger and garlic and pound together with the beancurd, soya sauce, sweet and sour sauce, sugar, salt and freshly ground white pepper. Pour the mixture over the ribs, place in the refrigerator and allow to marinate for 24 hours. After marination hang the pork on hooks and cook in a very hot charcoal oven for 25 minutes then remove, brush with the chilli sauce and return to the oven for a further 5 minutes. Remove the pork again and this time brush with the remaining marinade. Return to the oven for another 5 minutes or until the pork is fully cooked.

Note: If a charcoal oven is not available, cook the pork on a rack over a charcoal fire taking care to retain an even heat. When using this method turn the meat occasionally and baste with the sauce and marinade as above.

SPECIAL FRIED SPARERIBS

2 lb ribs of pork
2 eggs
2 Tbsp ginger juice
2 Tbsp Chinese wine
1/2 tsp Chinese five-spice powder
1/2 tsp salt
1/2 tsp white pepper
3 Tbsp cornstarch
2 brown onions
2 cloves garlic
oil for deep frying
1/3 cup tomato sauce
1/3 cup Worcestershire sauce
1/3 cup chicken stock
1 Tbsp light soya sauce
1 Tbsp dark soya sauce
5 Tbsp sugar

Trim excess fat from the ribs and cut into individual bones. Tap the bones lightly with the back of a knife (this loosens the meat a little) and cut each rib into two, then place in a shallow dish. Beat the eggs, add the ginger juice, wine, five-spice powder, salt, pepper and two-thirds of the cornstarch and mix well. Pour the mixture over the ribs and set aside for 2 hours. Chop the onions and crush the garlic. Heat the oil in a wok until it starts to smoke, then add the ribs and cook for 3-4 minutes. Remove the ribs and drain on kitchen paper. Pour away most of the oil, add the onion and garlic and stir-fry over a moderate heat for 2-3 minutes, then add the tomato sauce, Worcestershire sauce, stock, soya sauce and sugar and bring to the boil. Lower heat and stir until the sugar dissolves, then replace the ribs and continue to cook slowly for 5 minutes. Finally, mix the remaining cornstarch with a small quantity of cold water, stir into the sauce and bring back to the boil. Simmer for a further minute, then transfer to a serving dish.

Photo pages 44 & 45: *Sweet & Sour Pork*

PORK WITH GREEN PEPPERS

1¼ lbs pork loin
2 green peppers
1 brown onion
2 fresh red chillies
½ inch knob fresh ginger
2 cloves garlic
oil for deep-frying
1 Tbsp chilli bean paste
½ tsp sugar
2 Tbsp Chinese wine
1 Tbsp light soya sauce
1 tsp dark soya sauce
⅓ cup chicken stock
1 tsp cornstarch
2 tsp finely chopped spring onion

Place the pork in a pan of boiling water, cover and cook over a moderate heat until tender. Remove and allow to cool, then cut into thin slices. Slice the peppers, onion, chillies and ginger and crush the garlic. Heat the oil in a wok until it is almost smoking and deep-fry the pork until golden and crispy, then remove and drain on kitchen paper. Pour away most of the oil, add the onion, chilli, garlic and ginger and stir-fry for 3-4 minutes. Then, add the bean paste, sugar, wine, soya sauce and stock and bring to the boil. Reduce the heat and continue to cook for a further 2 minutes. Mix the cornstarch with a small quantity of cold water and add to the wok. Stir for 30 seconds, then transfer to a serving dish and garnish with finely chopped spring onion.

PEKING SHREDDED PORK

10 oz pork tenderloin
½ tsp salt
¼ tsp white pepper
1 egg white
2 tsp cornstarch
2 spring onions
2 cloves garlic
⅓ cup vegetable oil
1 tsp sugar
1 tsp Hoisin sauce
2 tsp light soya sauce
1 tsp dark soya sauce
2 tsp Chinese wine
⅓ cup chicken stock
fresh coriander

Cut the pork into fine shreds and season with salt and pepper. Beat the egg white and mix with half the cornstarch and a small quantity of cold water, then pour over the pork. Set aside for 15 minutes. Chop the spring onions and crush the garlic. Heat two-thirds of the oil in the wok and when very hot, add the pork and stir-fry for 1 minute then remove the meat and drain on kitchen paper. Add the remaining oil and replace the wok over a moderately hot heat, then add the spring onion and garlic and stir-fry for 2 minutes. Replace the pork, add the sugar, Hoisin sauce, soya sauce, wine and stock and bring to the boil then reduce the heat and cook for further 2 minutes. Mix the remaining cornstarch with a small quantity of cold water and stir into the pan. Increase the heat, cook for a further 30 seconds, then transfer to a serving dish and garnish with coriander.

Photo opposite page: *Peking Shredded Pork*

Lamb Apple Korma

MUTTON SHISH KEBABS

1 lb mutton
1 tsp salt
1/2 tsp white pepper
2 shallots
2 fresh red chillies
2 fresh green chillies
3/4 inch knob fresh ginger
3 cloves garlic
1 egg
2 tsp chopped parsley
2 tsp chopped mint
1/4 tsp powdered mace
1 Tbsp curry powder
3 Tbsp white breadcrumbs
2 Tbsp tomato sauce
2 Tbsp fresh lemon juice

Date Sauce:
4 oz dates
1 shallot
1 fresh red chilli
1 clove garlic
2 Tbsp soft brown sugar
2 Tbsp chilli sauce
salt to taste
freshly ground black pepper

Grind the mutton and season to taste with salt and white pepper. Chop the shallots, chillies and ginger very finely and crush the garlic. Place the shallots, chillies, ginger and garlic in a stone mortar and pound to a smooth paste. Transfer to a large mixing bowl, break in the egg, add the mutton, parsley, mint, mace, curry powder, breadcrumbs, tomato sauce and lemon juice and blend thoroughly. Dip the wooden kebab sticks in cold water and wet the hands then take a little of the mixture and shape it around a stick like a long thin sausage roll, about 3/4 inch thick and 4 inches in length. Press slightly with the hands. When all the kebabs have been prepared cook over a hot charcoal fire or under a grill until the meat is well cooked. Serve with the prepared date sauce.

To make the sauce: remove the stones from the dates and pass through a fine grinder. Chop the shallot, chilli, garlic and mint and pound these together with the dates. Add the brown sugar, chilli sauce, salt and pepper to taste and 1/3 cup of cold water. Continue to pound until the ingredients are thoroughly blended and the sauce is thick and smooth. Add a little more water if a thinner sauce is preferred. Serve as a dip for the kebabs.

LAMB APPLE KORMA

1 1/4 lbs lamb neck fillet
2 cooking apples
1 large brown onion
2 large ripe tomatoes
3 cloves garlic
3 Tbsp ghee
2 tsp coriander powder
2 tsp cumin powder
1 tsp chilli powder
2 Tbsp ground cashew nuts
1/3 cup natural yoghurt
salt to taste
freshly ground black pepper
3 Tbsp fresh cream

Trim excess fat from the lamb and cut into cubes. Peel and dice the apples and onion, mash the tomatoes and finely chop the garlic. Heat the ghee in a frying pan, add the onion and fry until golden. Then, add the apples, tomato, garlic, coriander and cumin and stir-fry for 5 minutes. Add the chilli powder and ground cashew nuts and cook for a further 3 minutes, then pour in the yoghurt and season to taste with salt and freshly ground pepper. Simmer for 5 minutes, stirring frequently, then add the lamb, pour in 1 cup of cold water and bring to the boil. Lower heat and cook slowly until the lamb is tender, approximately 45 minutes. Finally remove from heat, stir in the cream and serve immediately.

Beef Rendang

1 lb lean beef
6 shallots
3/4 inch knob fresh ginger
2 cloves garlic
4 fresh red chillies
2 tsp peanut oil
2 Tbsp vegetable oil
1 tsp sugar
3 Tbsp grated coconut
1 cup thick coconut milk
salt to taste

Cut the beef into bite-size pieces. Chop the shallots, ginger, garlic and chillies and pound together with the peanut oil to form a smooth paste. Heat the vegetable oil in a pan and fry the spice paste for 3-4 minutes, then add the sugar, grated coconut and coconut milk and bring to the boil. Lower heat, add the beef and salt to taste and simmer slowly until the beef is tender and most of the liquid has been absorbed. Serve with boiled rice or saffron rice.

Sliced Beef With Vegetables

14 oz lean beef
1/2 tsp salt
1/2 tsp black pepper
4 dried Chinese mushrooms
4 oz bamboo shoots
2 spring onions
2 cloves garlic
4 Tbsp peanut oil
2 Tbsp Chinese wine
1 Tbsp light soya sauce
1/3 cup beef stock
1 tsp cornstarch

Pound the beef, then cut into small slices and season with salt and pepper. Soak the mushrooms in warm water for 40 minutes, then discard the hard stems and slice the caps. Cover the bamboo shoots with cold water, bring to the boil and simmer for 3 minutes, then drain and cut into thin slices. Chop the spring onion into 3/4 inch lengths and crush the garlic. Heat the oil in a wok and stir-fry the beef for 1 minute, then remove and drain on kitchen paper. Add the mushroom, bamboo shoot, spring onion and garlic to the wok and stir-fry for 2 minutes over a high heat, then replace the beef, add the wine, soya sauce and stock and bring to the boil. Lower the heat and allow to simmer for a further 4-5 minutes. Finally, mix the cornstarch with a small quantity of cold water and stir into the sauce to thicken slightly.

Beef Balls With Cabbage

1 lb lean beef
1 brown onion
1 egg white
1 Tbsp Chinese wine
1 Tbsp light soya sauce
1 tsp dark soya sauce
freshly ground black pepper
1 Tbsp cornstarch
6 dried Chinese mushrooms
10 oz cabbage
3 Tbsp vegetable oil
2/3 cup beef stock
2 Tbsp finely chopped spring onion

Grind the beef and chop the onion very finely. Beat the egg white in a mixing bowl, add the beef, onion, wine, soya sauce, pepper and half the cornstarch and mix well. Shape into small balls and set aside. Soak the mushrooms in warm water for 40 minutes, then discard the hard stems and slice the caps. Shred the cabbage. Heat the oil in a wok and stir-fry the mushroom and cabbage for 2-3 minutes, then add the stock, adjust seasonings to taste and bring to the boil. Add the meat balls, cover with a tightly fitting lid and cook over a moderate heat for 20 minutes. Then, mix the remaining cornstarch with a small quality of cold water and stir into the sauce to thicken slightly. Transfer to a serving dish and garnish with the finely chopped spring onion.

BEEF WITH GREEN PEPPERS

14 oz lean beef steak
1 egg white
1 Tbsp dark soya sauce
2 Tbsp peanut oil
1 tsp cornstarch
$^1/_2$ tsp salt
$^1/_2$ tsp black pepper
2 green peppers
2 fresh red chillies
2 cloves garlic
$^1/_2$ cup vegetable oil
2 Tbsp Chinese wine
1 Tbsp light soya sauce
2 tsp oyster sauce
2 tsp sesame oil

Cut the beef into thin slices and place in a shallow dish. Beat the egg white, add the dark soya sauce, peanut oil, cornstarch, salt and pepper and pour over the beef. Set aside for 45 minutes. Chop the peppers, shred the chillies and crush the garlic. Heat the oil in a wok until it starts to smoke, then add the beef and fry for 30 seconds. Remove the beef and drain on kitchen paper. Pour away most of the oil from the wok, add the pepper, chilli and garlic and stir-fry for 2 minutes, then replace the beef. Add the wine, light soya sauce and oyster sauce and cook for a further 2 minutes, stirring frequently, then transfer to a serving dish. Finally, warm the sesame oil and sprinkle over the beef.

SLICED BEEF WITH OYSTER SAUCE

12 oz beef steak
1 egg white
2 tsp cornstarch
2 Tbsp Chinese wine
1 Tbsp light soya sauce
salt to taste
freshly ground black pepper
4 dried Chinese mushrooms
2 spring onions
1/2 inch knob fresh ginger
2 cloves garlic
3 Tbsp peanut oil
2 Tbsp oyster sauce

Cut the meat into thin bite-size slices and place in a shallow dish. Mix together the egg white, cornstarch, wine, soya sauce, salt and pepper, pour over the beef and set aside for 30 minutes. Soak the mushrooms in warm water for 30 minutes, discard the hard stems and cut the caps into thin strips. Chop the spring onions and ginger and crush garlic. Heat the oil in a wok, add the ginger, garlic and mushroom and stir-fry for 1 minute. Then, add the beef together with the marinade and bring to the boil. Add the oyster sauce and the spring onion and cook over a high heat for a further minute, stirring continuously.

Stalls' Food

HAINANESE CHICKEN RICE

1 chicken, approx 3¹/₄ lbs
1 tsp salt
1¹/₂ cups long-grain rice
2 inch cucumber
2 tomatoes
6 shallots
4 fresh red chillies
³/₄ inch knob fresh ginger
2 cloves garlic
fresh coriander leaves
freshly ground black pepper

Prepare the chicken, season both the inside and outside with salt and set aside for 1 hour. Wash the rice under cold running water, then drain thoroughly. Cut the cucumber and tomato into tiny dice, chop the shallots, chillies and ginger and crush the garlic. In a saucepan, bring 1¹/₂ quarts of water to the boil, add the ginger and garlic and allow to boil rapidly for 3-4 minutes. Then, add the chicken and the coriander leaves, cover the pan, and cook slowly until the chicken is tender. Remove a little oil from the surface of the cooking stock and set this aside. Remove the chicken, cut into small slices and arrange on a serving platter. Heat the reserved oil in a fresh saucepan and stir-fry the shallot for 3-4 minutes, then pour in half the cooking stock, add the cucumber, tomato and chilli, season with freshly ground black pepper and bring to the boil. Cover the pan, lower heat and allow to simmer for 20 minutes. Meanwhile, bring the remaining stock back to the boil, add the rice, cover the pan and cook until the rice is tender and fluffy. Transfer the soup and rice to individual serving bowls and place the platter of chicken in the centre of the table. Garnish the chicken with more coriander leaves and serve with side dishes of ginger and garlic sauce, chilli sauce and soya sauce.

OYSTER OMELETTE

1 lb small oysters
1 Tbsp Chinese wine
freshly ground black pepper
1 spring onion
1 fresh red chilli
1 clove garlic
6 celery leaves
3 Tbsp rice flour
¹/₄ tsp salt
5 eggs
2 Tbsp vegetable oil
2 tsp light soya sauce
1 tsp dark soya sauce

Open the oysters and remove from the shell. Wash under cold running water and drain thoroughly, then season with wine and freshly ground black pepper and set aside for 20 minutes. Chop the spring onion, chilli, garlic and celery leaves very finely. Mix the flour and salt with ³/₄ cup of warm water. Beat the eggs in a separate bowl. Heat the oil in a wok until it is very hot, then add the batter and egg. Stir to blend and allow to set slightly, breaking the mixture up with a spatula, then remove to the side of the wok. Add the oyster, onion, chilli, garlic and celery leaves and stir fry for 3-4 minutes. Add the soya sauce and adjust seasonings to taste, then bring the egg mixture back to the centre of the wok, stir to blend thoroughly and continue to cook until the egg is set.

Photo previous page: *Hainanese Chicken Rice*

FISH HEAD CURRY

1 large fish head
2 large brown onions
2 large tomatoes
4 fresh red chillies
2 fresh green chillies
1 inch knob fresh ginger
2 cloves garlic
3 Tbsp vegetable oil
2 Tbsp curry powder
2 curry leaves
2 Tbsp tamarind water
1¾ cups thin coconut milk
salt to taste

Wash the fish head under cold running water and pat dry. Slice the onions, quarter the tomatoes and finely chop the chillies, ginger and garlic. Mix the curry powder with a small quantity of cold water to form a smooth paste. Heat the oil in a large pan and fry the onion, ginger and garlic for 2-3 minutes, then add the chillies and continue to cook for a further 3 minutes, stirring frequently. Next, add the curry paste and the curry leaves, cover the pan and cook over a moderate heat for 2 minutes, then remove the lid and slowly pour in the tamarind water and the coconut milk, stirring to blend thoroughly. When simmering, add the fish head and the tomatoes and season to taste with salt. Cook for 8-10 minutes over a moderate head until the fish is completely cooked. Transfer the fish head to a serving plate and keep warm. Increase heat under the pan and reduce the sauce by one quarter, then pour this over the fish and serve with plain rice.

Note: In many 'Western' kitchens the fish head is used only for stock, or indeed may often by wastefully discarded, yet here is to be found some of the tastiest meat on the fish. So even though fish fillets could simply be substituted by the unadventurous for a similar result the recipe is highly recommended in its original form.

STUFFED CUTTLEFISH

12 medium size cuttlefish
12 oz chicken meat
2 shallots
2 spring onions
2 fresh red chillies
2 tsp blachan (shrimp paste)
1 Tbsp peanut oil
2 tsp sugar
salt to taste
freshly ground black pepper
1¼ cups thick coconut milk
2 tsp sesame oil

Clean the cuttlefish and remove the head, tentacles and backbone. Chop the chicken meat finely, season to taste and stuff into the cuttlefish. Chop the shallots, spring onions, chillies and blachan and pound these together. Heat the oil in a small pan and fry the pounded ingredients for 3 minutes, then add the sugar, salt and pepper and stir to blend thoroughly. Add the coconut milk, bring to simmering point and stir well for a further 2-3 minutes, then add the stuffed cuttlefish and simmer until tender, about 20 minutes. Transfer to a serving dish. Finally, warm the sesame oil and sprinkle on top.

SOUR SOUP NOODLES

10 oz rice vermicelli
1 1/2 lbs fish pieces, including head
salt to taste
freshly ground black pepper
6 fresh red chillies
1 stalk lemon grass
2 tsp blachan (shrimp paste)
2 large brown onions
1 tsp turmeric powder
1/2 small cucumber
3 slices pineapple
1 Tbsp sugar
3 Tbsp tamarind water
fresh mint leaves

Place the noodles in a pan of rapidly boling water for 1 minute, then remove the pan from the heat. Allow the noodles to stand for 2 minutes, then drain thoroughly and set aside. Place the pieces of fish in a large saucepan, cover with 1 1/2 quarts of water and bring to the boil. Season with salt and freshly ground black pepper, cover the pan and allow to simmer for 30 minutes. Pour the stock through a sieve into a fresh saucepan and set aside. Discard all the fish bones and skin and cut the remaining flesh into shreds. Chop the chillies, lemon grass, blachan and one of the onions and pound together with the turmeric powder and 2 teaspoons of the fish stock to form a smooth paste. Chop the cucumber, pineapple and remaining onion into small pieces. Bring the stock back to the boil, add the spice paste and sugar and stir to blend thoroughly. Add the shredded fish and tamarind water and adjust seasonings to taste. Allow to simmer for 5 minutes. To serve: place a portion of noodles into individual bowls, add pieces of onion, cucumber and pineapple and pour in the stock. Garnish with mint leaves.

SINGAPORE NOODLES

18 oz rice noodles
7 oz bean sprouts
7 oz shrimps
4 oz boiled squid
4 oz roasted pork
6 fresh red chillies
2 spring onions
2 cloves garlic
3 Tbsp peanut oil
1/3 cup chicken stock
salt to taste
freshly ground black pepper
2 tsp dark soya sauce
2 eggs
2 Tbsp fresh milk

Soak the noodles in a bowl of very hot water for 30 seconds, pour into a colander and drain thoroughly, then par-boil for 2 minutes. Wash and trim the bean sprouts. Shell and de-vein the shrimps and cut in half lengthways. Cut the squid and pork into thin strips. Chop the chillies and spring onions and crush the garlic. Heat half the oil in a wok and stir-fry the garlic for 1 minute, then add the chilli, shrimps, squid and pork and continue to stir-fry over a moderate heat for a further 3 minutes, placing a cover on the wok for the last minute. Then, remove the cover, pour in the stock, add the spring onion and season to taste with salt and freshly ground black pepper. Bring to the boil, add the bean sprouts and stir for 1 minute. Add the remaining oil, the soya sauce and the noodles and stir to blend thoroughly. Replace the cover on the wok and cook for 30 seconds, then transfer to a serving dish. Beat the eggs with the milk and pour into the wok. Place over a moderate heat and when the egg is set cut into thin strips and place on top of the noodles.

Singapore Noodles

SINGAPORE MEAT SATAY

14 oz beef or mutton
4 shallots
2 cloves garlic
4 small lemon grass
3/4 inch knob fresh ginger
1 tsp coriander powder
1 tsp cumin powder
2 tsp sugar
salt to taste
freshly ground black peper
peanut oil for basting

Satay sauce:
8 dried red chillies
2 cloves garlic
4 shallots
4 candlenuts (or macadamia nuts)
2 Tbsp thick coconut milk
3 Tbsp peanut oil
1 cup shelled peanuts
3 Tbsp tamarind water
2 Tbsp sugar
salt to taste
freshly ground black pepper

Cut the meat into small thin strips, about 2 inch x 3/4 inch. Chop the shallots, garlic, lemon grass and ginger and place in a stone mortar and pound together with the coriander and cumin. Transfer to a large bowl, add the meat, sugar, salt, freshly ground black pepper and 4 Tbsp of cold water. Mix with a wooden spoon to blend thoroughly and set aside for 1 hour. When marinated place the meat on wooden skewers (3 or 4 pieces to each skewer) and cook over a hot charcoal fire, basting frequently with the peanut oil. Serve with slices of raw onion, wedges of cucumber and satay sauce.

To make the sauce: first soak the chillies in cold water until they become soft then chop finely. Chop the garlic, shallots and macadamia nuts. Grind all these ingredients together with the coconut milk. Heat the oil in a large pan and stir-fry the spice paste for 5 minutes. Then chop the peanuts very finely and add these to the pan together with the tamarind water, 3/4 cup of cold water, the sugar, salt and freshly ground black pepper. Bring to the boil then lower heat and simmer slowly until the sauce thickens to a desired consistency.

SPICED MUTTON CHOPS

1¼ lb mutton chops
3 Tbsp Worcestershire sauce
1 Tbsp dark soya sauce
4 shallots
3 fresh red chillies
1 fresh green chilli
1 inch knob fresh ginger
3 cloves garlic
2 tsp curry powder
1 tsp coriander powder
2 Tbsp peanut oil
salt to taste
freshly ground white pepper
ghee for frying

Trim the excess fat from the chops and place in a shallow dish. Pour the Worcestershire sauce and soya sauce over the chops and set aside for 1 hour. Chop the shallots, chillies, ginger and garlic and pound together with the curry powder, coriander powder and peanut oil. Place the spice paste in a heavy saucepan and stir-fry for 2 minutes, then add the chops, season to taste with salt and freshly ground pepper and pour in just sufficient cold water to prevent the chops from sticking. Stir well then cover the pan and cook over a low heat until the chops are tender and the liquid has dried up. Just prior to serving heat the ghee in a frying pan and fry the chops for 2 minutes, turning once. Serve with steamed rice and a green salad.

MURTABA

8 oz beef
1 onion
1 small tomato
1 green chilli
2 Tbsp oil
¾ cup shelled peas
salt
freshly ground black pepper
1 egg
2½ cups wholewheat flour
3 Tbsp ghee

Grind the beef and finely chop the onion, tomato and chilli. Heat the oil in a pan and fry the onion for 1 minute then add the chilli, tomato, beef and peas and stir to mix well. Season to taste with salt and pepper and cook for 8-10 minutes. Lightly beat the egg. Mix the flour with sufficient water to make a stiff dough, then cover and set aside for 30 minutes. Knead until smooth, then divide into eight portions and roll out each as thinly as possible. Heat a quarter of the ghee on an iron griddle and fry each pancake for 1 minute, turning once, then remove and brush one side with the beaten egg. Divide the meat mixture into eight portions and spread on top of each pancake and fold over. Heat the remaining ghee in a clean pan and fry the pancakes until golden brown on both sides.

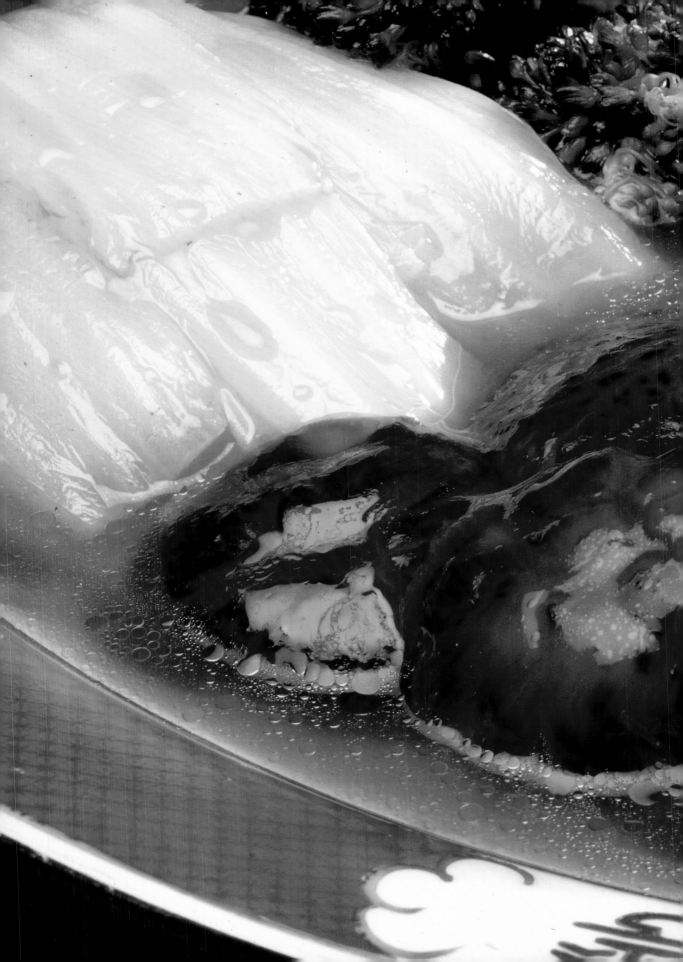

Vegetables

BRAISED ASSORTED VEGETABLES

6 dried Chinese mushrooms
10 oz Chinese cabbage
1/2 cup vegetable oil
4 oz button mushrooms
7 oz broccoli florets
1 cup chicken stock
salt to taste
4 slices fresh ginger
1/2 tsp sesame oil
2 Tbsp oyster sauce
2 Tbsp Chinese wine
2 Tbsp cornstarch

Soak the dried mushrooms in warm water for 30 minutes and discard the hard stems. Chop the cabbage into 8 pieces. Heat 2 Tbsp of oil in a wok and stir-fry the button mushrooms for 1 minute, then remove and set aside. Add a further 2 Tbsp of oil to the wok and stir-fry the broccoli for 45 seconds, then pour in 1/3 cup of stock, add a little salt and bring to the boil. Cover and cook for 2 minutes, then remove and set aside. In a fresh pan heat another 2 Tbsp of oil, add the cabbage and a little salt and stir-fry for 45 seconds, then add 1/2 cup of stock and the Chinese mushrooms and bring to the boil. Cover and cook over a moderate heat for 10 minutes, then remove, drain thoroughly and arrange on a serving dish together with the button mushrooms and broccoli. Heat the remaining oil in a wok, add the slices of ginger and stir-fry until they become dark brown, then discard. Pour the sesame oil, oyster sauce, wine and remaining stock into the wok and bring to the boil. Finally, mix the cornstarch with a small quantity of cold water and stir into the sauce. Adjust seasonings to taste and pour over the vegetables.

EGGPLANT IN HOT GARLIC SAUCE

12 oz eggplant
3 cloves garlic
3/4 inch knob fresh ginger
3 fresh red chillies
2 spring onions
3 Tbsp peanut oil
3 oz ground lean beef
1 Tbsp sugar
1 Tbsp Chinese wine
1 Tbsp light soya sauce
2 tsp dark soya sauce
1/2 cup chicken stock
salt to taste
freshly ground white pepper
2 tsp vinegar
1 tsp sesame oil

Trim and wash the eggplant and cut thin slices. Finely chop the garlic, ginger, chillies and spring onions. Heat the peanut oil in a wok and stir-fry the eggplant over a low heat for 2 minutes, then remove and squeeze out all excess oil. Pour away most of the oil from the wok, then add the garlic, ginger, chilli, onion and beef and stir-fry for 2 minutes. Add the sugar, wine, soya sauce and stock and bring to the boil. Replace the eggplant, season to taste with salt and pepper and cook until the liquid has reduced by two-thirds. Stir in the vinegar and sesame oil and transfer to a serving dish.

Photo previous page: *Braised Assorted Vegetables*

BRAISED ASSORTED MUSHROOMS

8 oz can golden mushrooms
4 oz can straw mushrooms
4 oz can button mushrooms
3 oz smoked ham
3 oz canned abalone
3 Tbsp vegetable oil
3 oz snow peas
2 tsp dark soya sauce
salt to taste
freshly ground black pepper
2 tsp Chinese wine
1 Tbsp crisply fried onion

Drain the mushrooms and reserve $1/3$ cup of the liquid. Shred the ham and cut the abalone into thin slices. Heat the oil in a wok and stir-fry the ham and abalone for 30 seconds, then add the mushrooms, snow peas, soya sauce, salt and pepper and continue to cook for a further minute. Pour in the reserved liquid and wine and bring to the boil, then lower the heat and cover. Allow to simmer for 3-4 minutes, then transfer to a serving dish and sprinkle the crisply fried onion on top.

STIR-FRIED MIXED VEGETABLES

1 brown onion
4 shallots
2 cloves garlic
1 cauliflower
6 carrots
3 fresh red chillies
1 green pepper
20 long green beans
12 ears baby corn
3 Tbsp peanut oil
$1/3$ cup tomato sauce
$1/3$ cup chilli sauce
salt to taste
freshly ground black pepper

Chop the onion, shallots and garlic and pound together to form a smooth paste. Break the cauliflower into florets, slice the carrots, chillies and green pepper and cut the beans into short lengths. Heat the oil in a large pan and stir-fry the onion-paste for 3-4 minutes, then, add the vegetables and stir-fry for 5-6 minutes. Add the tomato sauce and chilli sauce, season to taste with salt and freshly ground black pepper and continue to cook for a further 2-3 minutes, stirring frequently. Serve immediately.

CURRIED POTATO WITH ONION

1 lb potatoes
$1/4$ tsp salt
$1/4$ turmeric powder
$1/2$ tsp paprika
1 tsp curry powder
2 large brown onions
$1/2$ tsp mustard seeds
$1/3$ cup vegetable oil
3 curry leaves
$3/4$ inch stick cinnamon
1 tsp fresh lemon juice

Boil the potatoes, cut into bite-size chunks and season with salt, turmeric powder, paprika and curry powder. Slice the onions and grind the mustard seeds. Heat the oil and when very hot, add the curry leaves, onion, mustard and cinnamon stick. Stir-fry until the onions are golden brown, then add the potato. Continue to cook, stirring frequently, until the potato is brown and hot. Remove the cinnamon stick and curry leaves, then transfer to a serving dish and sprinkle the lemon juice on top.

MIXED VEGETABLE CURRY

2 potatoes
2 tomatoes
4 carrots
5 oz green beans
1 small cauliflower
2 shallots
3/4 inch knob fresh ginger
2 cloves garlic
2 fresh red chillies
3 Tbsp ghee
1/2 tsp turmeric powder
1/2 tsp coriander powder
1/4 tsp cumin powder
1/2 cup natural yoghurt
salt to taste
freshly ground black pepper

Wash and prepare all the vegetables. Par-boil the potatoes and cut into medium-size dice. Slice the tomatoes, carrots and beans and break the cauliflower into florets. Chop finely the shallots, ginger, garlic and chillies. Heat the ghee in a large pan and stir-fry the shallots, ginger and garlic for 3-4 minutes. Add the turmeric, coriander and cumin powder and stir well, then add the potato, carrot and beans and stir-fry for 2-3 minutes over a high heat. Pour in the yoghurt and bring to the boil. Add the tomato, cauliflower and chillies and season to taste with salt and freshly ground black pepper. Lower heat, stir to blend thoroughly and allow to simmer until the vegetables are cooked and most of the liquid has been absorbed.

Note: Take care not to overcook the vegetables.

DAL CURRY

1 lb red dal (lentils)
3 brown onions
1 tsp turmeric powder
2 fresh red chillies
3/4 inch knob fresh ginger
2 cloves garlic
2 tomatoes
1/2 tsp coriander seeds
1/2 tsp cumin seeds
2 Tbsp vinegar
3 Tbsp ghee
1 tsp garam masala
1/4 tsp salt
1 tsp freshly chopped coriander leaves

Place the dal in a saucepan. Chop one of the onions finely and add to the dal. Cover with cold water and bring to the boil. Add the turmeric powder, lower heat, and simmer until the dal is soft, then remove from heat and set aside. Slice the remaining 2 onions and chop finely the chillies, ginger and garlic. Chop the tomatoes. Grind the chilli, ginger, garlic, cumin and coriander seeds and blend with the vinegar to form a smooth spice paste. Heat the ghee in a pan and fry the sliced onion until soft and translucent, then add the spice-paste and cook for 5 minutes, stirring frequently. Add the mixture to the dal and place over a moderate heat. Add the chopped tomato and season with garam masala and salt. Stir to blend thoroughly and allow to simmer for 3-4 minutes, then transfer to a serving dish and sprinkle the chopped coriander on top.

Photo opposite page: *Mixed Vegetables & Dal Curries*

CHILLI BEANCURD WITH PORK

14 oz fresh beancurd
5 oz fresh pork
4 red chillies
2 shallots
2 cloves garlic
1/3 cup peanut oil
1 tsp hot bean paste
2 tsp dark soya sauce
2 tsp Chinese wine
1 cup chicken stock
salt
freshly ground white pepper
2 tsp finely chopped spring onion

Soak the beancurd in cold water for 2 minutes, then drain and cut into bite-size pieces. Grind or finely chop the pork. Chop the chillies and shallots and crush the garlic. Heat the oil in a wok and stir-fry the pork for 3-4 minutes, then remove and drain. Add the chilli, shallot and garlic to the wok and stir-fry for 3 minutes then replace the pork, add the bean paste, soya sauce, wine and stock and bring to the boil. Lower heat, add the beancurd and season to taste with salt and pepper. Cook slowly for 3-4 minutes, then transfer to a serving dish and sprinkle the finely chopped spring onion on top.

MUSHROOMS WITH BEANCURD

6 dried Chinese mushrooms
14 oz fresh beancurd
1 shallot
³/₄ inch knob fresh ginger
1 clove garlic
oil for deep frying
1 Tbsp Chinese wine
1 Tbsp light soya sauce
2 tsp dark soya sauce
¹/₂ cup chicken stock
2 tsp sugar
freshly ground black pepper
2 tsp cornstarch

Soak the mushrooms in warm water for 40 minutes, then discard the hard stems and halve the caps. Cut the beancurd into bite-size pieces and finally chop the shallot, ginger and garlic. Heat the oil in a large wok until it starts to smoke, then deep-fry the beancurd until the outside is golden. Remove the beancurd and drain on kitchen paper. Pour away all but ¹/₃ cup of the oil and replace the wok over a moderate heat. Add the mushroom, shallot, ginger and garlic and stir-fry for 2-3 minutes, then add the wine, soya sauce, stock, sugar and pepper and bring to the boil. Replace the beancurd, cover and allow to simmer over a moderate heat for a further 2-3 minutes. Finally, mix the cornstarch with a small quantity of cold water and stir into the sauce to thicken slightly.

Desserts

CARROT HALWA

1 lb carrots
2½ cups fresh milk
1 cup sugar
3 Tbsp melted butter
2 Tbsp sliced almonds
2 Tbsp chopped pistachios
2 Tbsp seedless raisins
¼ tsp saffron powder

Wash and scrape carrots, then grate finely and place in a saucepan. Add two thirds of the milk together with three quarters of the sugar and slowly bring to the boil. Allow to simmer, stirring frequently, until all the milk has been absorbed. Dissolve the remaining sugar with some warm water and add to the mixture. Boil the remaining milk and allow to reduce to one quarter, then add this to the pan also. Stir well and continue to cook over a low heat for 3-4 minutes, until the mixture is of a very thick consistency. Add the butter, almonds, pistachios and raisins, stir to blend thoroughly and cook until the mixture turns a deep golden brown. Sprinkle a little saffron powder on top and serve immediately.

SWEET SAGO PUDDING

7 oz sago
⅔ cup unsalted cashew nuts
¾ cup golden raisins
¾ cup thick coconut milk
¾ cup date-palm sugar
¼ tsp salt

Wash the sago under cold running water and drain well. Pour 1 cup of water into a saucepan and place over moderate heat. When the water is just at the boil, sprinkle in the sago and simmer until the sago becomes transparent, approximately 8-10 minutes. Add the cashew nuts and sultanas and continue to simmer for 7-8 minutes. Then, add the coconut milk, sugar and salt, bring back to the boil and stir until the sugar has completely dissolved. Spoon into individual dishes and sprinkle a little rose essence on top of each. Serve either hot or cold.

Photo previous page: *Carrot Halwa*

PEANUT PUDDING

¹/₃ cup peanut oil
1 cup fresh peanuts
²/₃ cup cornstarch
3 Tbsp condensed milk
³/₄ cup granulated white sugar
2 tsp soft brown sugar

Heat the oil in a pan and stir-fry the peanuts for 3 minutes, then pour into a colander and allow to cool. Remove skins from the peanuts and grind very finely. Mix the cornstarch with a small quantity of cold water. In a saucepan heat 3 cups of water and when just coming to the boil add the ground peanuts and stir. Add the cornstarch, condensed milk and white sugar and simmer over a moderate heat for 4 minutes, stirring frequently. Transfer to individual serving dishes and sprinkle a little brown sugar on top.

PEANUT PANCAKES

1¹/₄ cups flour
¹/₂ tsp baking powder
¹/₄ tsp salt
5 Tbsp caster sugar
2 eggs
1¹/₄ cups milk
oil for frying
³/₄ cup finely chopped roasted peanuts
6 Tbsp soft butter

Sift the flour, baking powder, salt and half the sugar into a mixing bowl and make a well in the centre. Beat the eggs lightly and pour into the well, together with one third of the milk. Stir well, then gradually add the remaining milk and continue stirring to produce a smooth batter. Set aside in a cool place for 30 minutes. Pour a little oil into a heavy based frying pan, place over a fairly high heat and pour in sufficient batter to coat the bottom of the pan. Cover and cook until the pancake is almost ready, then sprinkle on some chopped peanuts and spread a little butter on top. Fold over and finish cooking, turning sonce so that the pancake is golden on both sides. Remove, wrap in foil and keep warm, then repeat the process with the remaining batter. When all the pancakes are cooked, arrange on a serving plate and sprinkle the remaining sugar on top.

COCONUT CUSTARD

³/₄ cup date-palm sugar
10 eggs
1 cup thick coconut milk

Place the date-palm sugar in a saucepan, add ³/₄ cup of cold water and bring to the boil. Stir until the sugar has completely dissolved, then remove from heat and allow to cool. Break the eggs into a large ovenproof bowl and beat lightly. Add the coconumt milk and the syrup and stir to blend thoroughly, then place the bowl in a pan with a tightly fitting lid and steam over rapidly boiling water for 30-40 minutes. Serve immediately or allow to cool.

RUM-RAISIN ICE CREAM

1 fresh vanilla bean
1³/₄ cups milk
1 egg
5 egg whites
¹/₂ cup fine white sugar
¹/₂ cup fresh cream
¹/₂ cup dark rum
1¹/₄ cups seedless raisins
4 young coconuts
2 Tbsp grated coconut

Slice the vanilla bean and with a knife remove the seeds. Pour the milk into a saucepan, add the vanilla seeds and bring to the boil. Beat the egg and egg whites together wlth the sugar and add to the milk. Continue to simmer until the mixture thickens but do not allow to come to the boil again. Remove the pan from the heat, stir in the cream and allow the mixture to cool, then strain through a fine muslin cloth into an ice-cream maker. Place in the freezer compartment and when half set remove and fold in the rum and two thirds of the raisins. Return to the freezer until completely set. To serve: remove the tops from the coconuts, pour away any liquid and place scoops of ice-cream inside. Sprinkle the grated coconut and the remaining raisins on top.

PINEAPPLE CHEESECAKE

6 oz wheatmeal biscuits
3 Tbsp soft brown sugar
¹/₂ tsp cinnamon powder
6 Tbsp soft butter
10 oz cream cheese
8 oz sour cream
2 Tbsp pineapple juice
1 tsp gelatine powder
4 egg whites
2 Tbsp caster sugar
10 oz can pineapple rings
whipped cream
maraschino cherries

Crush the biscuits and mix with the brown sugar and cinnamon powder. Melt the butter, add the crushed biscuits and blend thoroughly, then spread the mixture evenly on the bottom and along the sides of a cake tin. Place in the refrigerator for 1 hour. Place the cream cheese and sour cream in a large bowl and mix well. Warm the pineapple juice in a saucepan, add the gelatine and stir until the gelatine has melted, then allow to cool before adding to the cream cheese. Beat the egg whites with the caster sugar until stiff, then fold into the mixture. Spoon the mixture into the prepared crust and place in a pre-heated moderately hot oven. Bake for 15-20 minutes, then turn off the oven and leave the cake standing inside for approximately 1 hour until the centre is firm. Allow to cool, then cut pineapple rings into thirds and arrange attractively on top of the cake. Decorate with cream and cherries.

FRIED BANANAS

8 small bananas
³/₄ cup flour
2 Tbsp soft butter
2 tsp fresh lemon juice
2 tsp fresh orange juice
2 Tbsp fine white sugar
2 Tbsp grated coconut

Peel the bananas and cut into quarters, first lengthways then across. Mix the flour with sufficient water to form a thin batter and coat the pieces of banana. Melt the butter in a frying pan and fry the banana pieces until golden on one side. Then turn over, add the lemon and orange juice and continue to cook until golden all over. Transfer to a serving dish and sprinkle the sugar and grated coconut on top.

Fried Bananas

Index